CAMBRIDGE LIBRARY COLLECTION

Books of enduring scholarly value

Archaeology

The discovery of material remains from the recent or the ancient past has always been a source of fascination, but the development of archaeology as an academic discipline which interpreted such finds is relatively recent. It was the work of Winckelmann at Pompeii in the 1760s which first revealed the potential of systematic excavation to scholars and the wider public. Pioneering figures of the nineteenth century such as Schliemann, Layard and Petrie transformed archaeology from a search for ancient artifacts, by means as crude as using gunpowder to break into a tomb, to a science which drew from a wide range of disciplines - ancient languages and literature, geology, chemistry, social history - to increase our understanding of human life and society in the remote past.

The Temple of the Andes

Richard Inwards (1840–1937) won renown as the author of the highly popular *Weather Lore* (also reissued in the Cambridge Library Collection). For many years he worked as a mine manager, and in 1866, while working in Bolivia, he visited the site of Tiwanaku. Although the ruins of this once great city were first described by the conquistadores, it was not until the nineteenth century, with the development of more rigorous archaeological methods, that the site began to be more fully studied. Although published in 1884, this brief account is based on Inwards' 1866 visit, and so is contemporaneous with the work there by E.G. Squier. Pre-dating many of the earliest studies, the book is well illustrated with sketches and plans. The text describes the structures that Inwards observed, provides current thinking as to their possible purpose and original characteristics, and also offers remarks on the local people and culture of the present day.

Cambridge University Press has long been a pioneer in the reissuing of out-of-print titles from its own backlist, producing digital reprints of books that are still sought after by scholars and students but could not be reprinted economically using traditional technology. The Cambridge Library Collection extends this activity to a wider range of books which are still of importance to researchers and professionals, either for the source material they contain, or as landmarks in the history of their academic discipline.

Drawing from the world-renowned collections in the Cambridge University Library and other partner libraries, and guided by the advice of experts in each subject area, Cambridge University Press is using state-of-the-art scanning machines in its own Printing House to capture the content of each book selected for inclusion. The files are processed to give a consistently clear, crisp image, and the books finished to the high quality standard for which the Press is recognised around the world. The latest print-on-demand technology ensures that the books will remain available indefinitely, and that orders for single or multiple copies can quickly be supplied.

The Cambridge Library Collection brings back to life books of enduring scholarly value (including out-of-copyright works originally issued by other publishers) across a wide range of disciplines in the humanities and social sciences and in science and technology.

The Temple of the Andes

RICHARD INWARDS

CAMBRIDGE
UNIVERSITY PRESS

University Printing House, Cambridge, CB2 8BS, United Kingdom

Cambridge University Press is part of the University of Cambridge.

It furthers the University's mission by disseminating knowledge in the pursuit of
education, learning and research at the highest international levels of excellence.

www.cambridge.org
Information on this title: www.cambridge.org/9781108077637

© in this compilation Cambridge University Press 2015

This edition first published 1884
This digitally printed version 2015

ISBN 978-1-108-07763-7 Paperback

THE

TEMPLE OF THE ANDES.

BY

RICHARD INWARDS, F.R.A.S., F.R. Met. Soc.

AUTHOR OF "WEATHER-LORE."

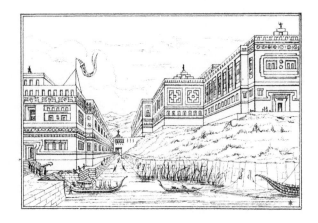

London : Printed for the Author by Vincent Brooks, Day & Son,

Lithographers to the Queen.

1884

PREFACE.

TO give an account of the ruins of an interesting ancient temple in Bolivia, and to show their connection with the history and traditions of the Peruvian people are the objects of this little book.

Most South American travellers are agreed that these ruins are the oldest in the New World, and that they show evidences of greater advancement in the arts than are seen in any other relics in the Western Hemisphere.

They will be shown to have curious points of resemblance to the ancient Egyptian works, and to be intimately connected with the early and primitive religion of Peru under the Incas.

The accounts of the old Spanish writers are drawn upon to throw light on the probable signification of the monuments, and some attempt is made to revive an interest in the aboriginal inhabitants of this magnificent country, so long racked by war and revolution.

The temple of Tiahuanaco was dedicated to the Creator.

THE
TEMPLE OF THE ANDES.

THOSE who have read the story of the conquering of Peru, so ably told in the pages of Prescott,[*] will not need to be reminded that, as a mixture of plain told truth and that which seems to be the wildest romance, it has scarcely a parallel in the history of the world. The unexpected, the unlikely, and the true are there, so smoothly blended into sober history that the reader scarcely knows whether he is most charmed with the story itself, or delighted with the way it is told.

If, in the middle ages, a man of imagination had thought fit to invent an account of a foreign land, for the purpose of decoying from Europe the adventurous and the unruly, he could not have told them a more glowing tale than the description of the high lands of Peru, which were then being conquered for them by Pizarro. A land fertile beyond belief, and teeming with new and delicious fruits; a people obedient by instinct, and to whom idleness was a crime; abounding with gold; ignorant of iron; easy to conquer, and faithful to death when brought under subjection; their temples plated with solid gold; their flocks and herds covered with strange and silky wool, and their mines of the precious metals, fabulous in number and in wealth—the account of all this might well have seemed a cunning fable and a snare. But it would have been true; and, however much one may now deplore the way in which a fine race has been almost civilised to extinction, one cannot help admiring the grand measure of hope and endurance shown by the early conquerors of the country, who, without knowing either the path or the language, and in the face of numbers

---

[*] History of the Conquest of Peru, by William H. Prescott.

at least a thousand-fold their own, forced their way in, carrying with them the Spanish Flag and the Cross, signals which were unhappily to be followed by unnumbered woes and scourges to the simple people who had so long dwelt in calm behind their mountains.

After Pizarro had, by what can only be called an act of daring brigandage, exacted the ransom of his prisoner, the Inca, and then, in defiance of even the brigand's code, murdered instead of releasing his captive,* he found the subjugation of the country comparatively easy. The people were like bees without a queen, and seemed unable to make any but the most feeble resistance when deprived of their chief. They were divided into two great classes—the one consisting of the nobles, or those related to the royal race; and the other of the common people. One class ruled while the other toiled. The people were without money, and the government was of the most fatherly kind. Everything was regulated so as to leave no room for independent action on the part of the subject race. They were nourished, clothed, and housed by the State; and, on arriving at the proper age, the men were even provided with wives, and given a piece of land on which to establish their little homes. Mildness, docility, and honesty were their leading characteristics. Their discipline was shown when, at the capture of the Inca, hundreds of them submitted to be slaughtered without striking a blow, because they had not received the word of command. Their habitual honesty was well shown, by the fact that no one attempted to steal the plates of beaten gold, with which the outsides of some of their temples were profusely adorned.

The one unfortunate weakness which caused such evil to the Peruvian race, was the fondness of the ruling class for vessels and ornaments of gold and silver. They were lavish in their use of these metals, and enormous quantities were seized by the invaders. Had it not been for this, Pizarro's expedition

---

* I cannot resist giving the names of those followers of Pizarro who protested against this crime. Most of the names are still borne by modern inhabitants of the South of Spain.

| Blas de Atienza. | Pedro de Ayala. | Fernando de Haro. | Diego de Mora. |
| Alonzo de Avila. | Diego de Chaves. | Juan de Herrada. | Francisco Moscoso. |

These names do not appear in the list of those who divided the plunder. The following, though protesting against the murder, appear as sharers of the ransom:—

| Francisco de Chaves. | Francisco de Fuentes. | Hernando de Soto. | Pedro de Mendoza. |

It is true, as Mr. C. R. Markham remarks, that the former may have been Almagro's men, who are not individually named in the list, but who took their share in a lump. However, if there were any men who refused to touch the Inca's gold, they will be in this first list. The names are taken from a true account of the Province of Cuzco, by Francisco Xeres, Salamanca, 1547, translated by Clements R. Markham, C.B., for the Hakluyt Society, 1872.

would have contented itself with colonisation and conversion, and so have proved a blessing to the native races, though it would have been regarded as a failure at the time. But the sight of so much gold turned these hardy adventurers into mere robbers, and they soon sacrificed the lives of the Indians in enormous numbers, by compelling them to work the mines of the country at a greedy and fatal rate.

The natives have steadily diminished in numbers ever since, and those now occupying the soil must be regarded as the patient survivals of the lower or labouring section of the Inca's subjects, as it is more than probable that the whole of the noble or ruling race have already perished, as being the principal competitors for empire with whom the foreign invaders had to deal. No native American race can be compared to the Peruvians for advancement in the arts, or for order, discipline, or morality. Their buildings, roads, and bridges ; their inland system of swift postal messengers, their order of knighthood, and elaborate court ceremones, must have brought the invaders face to face with a surprising reflection of the civilisation they had left behind them in the East.

It is necessary to mention, too, their system of religion, as it will have to be shown that the ruins about to be described are intimately connected with their scheme of worship, as well as with their most sacred traditions and the early history of their kings. There is, perhaps, no more surprising fact in connection with the discovery of America than the existence there of a fully-developed religious system, so analogous in many points to the higher forms of faith whieh have flourished in the Eastern Hemisphere. These Indians had churches, priests, sacrifices, altars, images, convents, baptisms, sacraments, prayers, and traditions, with all the complicated mechanism of worship in full operation amongst them, without consciousness that they were repeating the phases of growth of many of the systems already in existence.

The ancient Peruvians have generally been considered merely as sun-worshippers, but in reality they were nature worshippers, adoring the Creator, the sun, the moon, and the thunder, and, probably, in a greater or less degree, all the elements and powers of nature. They also venerated their own ancestors, and, as Molina says,* " whenever anything excelled all the rest of its kind in " beauty, they worshipped it, and made it huaca, or sacred."

---

* Molina. Account of the Fables and Rites of the Incas. Translated by Clements R. Markham, C.B., F.R.S., Hakluyt Society, 1873.

He also tells us, that in sacrificing the animals (which were to be without blemish), the order observed was—first one to the Creator, then to the Thunder, and then to the Sun.

That they gave to the Creator the first place in their religious system is shown by an anecdote told by Garcilasso de la Vega,* of one of their Incas, who, when reproved by the high priest for gazing upon the sun, turned to the priest and asked if it were true that not one of the Inca's subjects dared to disobey, even though despatched to the remotest parts of Chile. The priest was obliged to reply that the subject would obey the command, even unto death. "Then," said the Inca, "I perceive that there must be some other more powerful Lord, whom our Father the Sun esteems as much greater than himself, by whose command he every day measures the compass of the heavens without resting. If he were indeed the Supreme Lord, he would occasionally go aside from his course, or rest for his pleasure."

It seems clear from the accounts of the early missionaries, who took pains to find out from native priests all the ceremonies and precepts of their religion, that the Inca's people worshipped a Supreme Being, whom they knew by the name of Pacha Camac, a word equivalent, in their language, to " the soul of the " universe," and to whom they addressed prayers, some of which would not do discredit to any system of religion whatever. The following is a concise example of the kind :—" O, Creator, and Sun and Thunder, be for ever young! " Do not grow old. Let all things be at peace! Let the people multiply and " their food, and let all things continue to increase."† This was a prayer used during the month of May, at the approach of their winter, and there is something pathetic in their simple appeal to the Sun not to grow old, as it was then that he seemed to get lower in the sky and make a shorter journey, and they seem to have regarded this as a possible sign of age and weakness.

Mr. C. R. Markham aptly says on this subject :—" In all this we may " discern the popular religion of the Andean people, which consisted in the belief " that all things in nature had an ideal or soul, which ruled and guided them, " and to which men might pray for help."‡ They also believed in rewards and punishments after death, and, after the manner of the Egyptians, carefully

* Garcilasso de la Vega. Royal Commentaries of the Incas. Translated and edited by Clements R. Markham, Esq., C.B., F.R.S. For the Hakluyt Society, 1871.

† Rites and Laws of the Incas, p. 16.

‡ Narratives of the Rites and Laws of the Incas. Translated by Clements R. Markham, C.B., F.R.S. Hakluyt Society, 1873.

embalmed their dead, and buried with them gold and treasures for their delight in a future world.

They were not destitute of imagination, as witnessed their name for the planet Venus, signifying—The youth with flowing golden locks.

Their various names, too, for the Deity, signifying—" The Soul of the " World," " The Teacher of the Universe," " The Incomprehensible God," " The " Conquering Vira Cocha," show some clear conceptions of the subject.*

One is inclined to agree with the quaint remark of Acosta, as given in Grimstone's translation :—

"Although the darknesse of infidelitie holdeth these nations in blindnesse, yet in many things the light " of truth and reason works somewhat in them."†

Another prayer which they addressed to the Supreme Being deserves quotation :—‡

" O, Creator [O, Conquering Vira Cocha, ever present Vira Cocha], " Thou who art without equal unto the ends of the earth! Thou who givest " life and strength to mankind, saying : Let this be a man and let this be a " woman ; and as Thou sayest, so Thou givest life and vouchsafest that men shall " live in health and peace, and free from danger. Thou who dwellest in the " heights of heaven, in the thunder and in the storm-clouds, hear us! and grant " us eternal life. Have us in Thy keeping, and receive this our offering as it " shall please Thee, O Creator."

There is a fine breadth about this petition which might seem fitted for the use of the whole human race, and not merely of a small nation, occupying a few hundred square miles in one of the remotest corners of the earth.

Some sentences in their prayers it would be difficult to improve, such as " Keep Thy poor servants in health," " Make them and their children to walk " in a straight road without thinking any evil."

A passage from the Royal Commentaries, by Garcilasso de la Vega, who was himself descended from the Incas, will serve to show how far the ancient rulers strove to do good to their people :—§

" The Inca Manco Capac, in establishing his people in villages, while he

* Rites and Laws. Int , p. x.
   Natural and Moral History of the Indies. By Father Joseph de Acosta. Translated by Ed. Grimstone. Edited by C. R. Markham, C.B., F.R.S. Hakluyt Society, 1880.
   ‡ Molina, p. 28.
   § Garcilasso de la Vega. Book 1, chapter xxi. From the translation of C. R. Markham, Eso., C.B., F.R.S. Hakluyt Society, 1869.

B

" taught them to cultivate the land, to build houses, construct channels for irri-
" gation, and to do all other things necessary for human life, also instructed
" them in the ways of polite and brotherly companionship, in conformity with
" reason and the law of nature, persuading them with much earnestness to pre-
" serve perpetual peace and concord between themselves, and not to entertain
" anger or passionate feelings towards each other, but to do to one another as
" they would others should do to them, not laying down one law for themselves
" and another for their neighbours."

The same author also gives the following account of the tradition of
" Our Father the Sun " (as he was styled) giving his charge to the first Inca :—*

" When you have reduced these people to our service, you shall maintain
" them in habits of reason and justice, by the practice of piety, clemency, and
" meekness, assuming in all things the office of a pious father towards his
" beloved and tender children. Thus you will form a likeness and reflection of
" me. I do good to the whole world, giving light that men may see and do
" their business, making them warm when they are cold, cherishing their pastures
" and crops, ripening their fruits and increasing their flocks, watering their lands
" with dew, and bringing fine weather in the proper season. I take care to go
" round the earth each day, that I may see the necessities that exist in the world,
" and supply them, as the sustainer and benefactor of the heathens. I desire
" that you shall imitate this example as my children, sent to the earth solely for
" the instruction and benefit of those men who live like beasts. And from this
" time I constitute and name you as kings and lords over all the tribes, that
" you may instruct them in your rational works and government."

But, although there is good reason to believe that the old religion of the
Peruvians consisted in the purer kind of worship indicated by those ancient
teachings, yet it cannot be denied that when the Spaniards conquered the
country, this foundational religion had become overladen with ceremonies and
encumbered with many complicated rites and observances. It was not even
free from the taint of the actual worship of idols and even of occasional human
sacrifices.

It remains to say a few words about the Indians as they are, before
describing what remains of the temple dedicated by their forefathers to the
" All-Conquering Vira Cocha, the Teacher of the Universe."

* Book 1 Royal Commentaries.

In 1866, I was sent to Bolivia by that fine old firm of princely merchants, Messrs. Evans and Askin,* of Birmingham, who had cobalt mines on the steep side of Mount Sorata, almost at the limit of perpetual snow, in the very heart of the Aymará Indian country.

Here I passed about a year, and although I have since wandered wide and far in the other three-quarters of the globe, nothing has ever effaced, or in any way equalled, the impression made on my mind by the stupendous natural features of this magnificent country.

During this residence amongst the Indians, I had a good opportunity of observing the character, habits, and language of the people; and in one of my journeys to Lake Titicaca I was able to make the various sketches presented to the reader in this book.

The typical Indian of to-day is a light brown, middle-sized man, with an enormous chest, and with long, straight black hair, generally plaited in a long tail, which hangs down his back. He is tough and yet elastic; rarely looks in one's face; speaks little; seems never surprised; patient, obedient, enduring; temperate, frugal, and capable of sustaining life on the coarsest and scantiest food. He is addicted to chewing coca, and, indeed, is so much a slave to the habit that he cannot work or go a journey unless supplied with this stimulant. He is much skilled in the management of the herds of sheep and llamas, the latter animals having served for ages as the best beasts of burden for his mountain paths.

The Aymará Indian of the present may be looked on as a pattern of the passive and suffering class of virtues; his spirit is quelled; all the nobler portion of his nature seems to have been "bred out," under the influences of war, pestilence, or oppressive rule, so that it is no wonder if one fails to meet with few signs of his being the relic of a finer people. He is doggedly submissive to the powers, whatever they are, and conforms to the Christian religion with the same sort of wondering reverence that his ancestors seemed to have offered to the sun, the thunder, and the elements.

The modern traveller who would form a correct idea of the land of the Incas, should, as far as possible, pass over the country in the track of the early invaders. Landing upon the northern coast, he would find himself at first upon

* Now Henry Wiggin and Company.

a vast tract of sand, stretching more than a thousand miles to the south, and having the Pacific on one side and the Andes upon the other. At intervals of about a hundred miles, there would be small streams trickling through the sand during a few months of the year ; and on the banks of these streams he would see narrow patches of great fertility, water being the only thing wanted here to convert this desert into a garden. He would look in vain for rain on this coast, which, except the ribbons of verdure by the side of the scant streams, offers no home for beast, bird, or plant. One can understand the blank disappointment which must have seized on Pizarro's crew when they first landed on this desert, and before they had penetrated to the richer country beyond. Let the traveller now cross this waste of wearying sand—fortunate if escaping a hot whirlwind or an earthquake—and after journeying from ten to a hundred miles, according to the place chosen for his starting point, reaching at last the foot of the range of mountains, where he will soon find the picture changed. As the narrow road writhes in among the mountain spurs, he will see at every turn more and more fertility—first clover and maize, then sugar-canes and palms, until, on reaching a well-watered spot, he will find himself, although still in a comparatively rainless district, amongst the most luxuriant and beautiful products of the earth. Let him journey on, still up through the mountain passes, perhaps crossing by a slender rope bridge over a roaring river, hundreds of feet below him—such as that over the *Apu-rimac*, the "Great Speaker"—and so forward and still up to the rocky gateways of the Outer Andes, where new scenes await him. First, salt plains and sulphurous rivers ; then wide stretches of scant pasture, where there seems room enough for the flocks of the world to roam, and where the armies of the Incas marched along their well-made roads to the subjugation of all the valleys round, still on and up to a plain, which is 12,000 feet above the coast below, and passing the old capital of the country, the City of Cuzco, perched two miles in the air, in a spot well-chosen as the natural throne from which the whole land could be ruled, he will, after still more climbing, at last have before him a sight which well might have impressed its stamp upon the early religion of the people. Stretched away to the right and left, far as the eye can reach, is a blue lake, like another ocean, and beyond this again, the towering peaks of the great inner range of the Andes, mirroring themselves in the water, and throwing into littleness all the lesser heights that the traveller has yet toiled up in his journey.

Sailing along the lake on the reed-boats of the Indians, the traveller will, in a few days, arrive at its southern end, where it forms itself into a river, flowing gently into another lake, but neither having any further outlet, forming in this respect a parallel to the case of the Dead Sea and the Sea of Galilee, but with the remarkable difference that these Western waters are the highest large lakes in the world, while the Eastern ones are the very lowest. It is as if Nature had sought to compensate her disturbances.

Were the journey pursued but a few miles further, the traveller would reach the finger-tips of some of the myriad arms which (Briareus-like) the great Amazon is stretching out towards the Andes, and which would soon direct him by rapid downward steps—counted by cataracts, and each marked by a new climate and vegetation—to the humid forests, which are darkly spread away for thousands of untrodden miles towards the Atlantic.

But already at the south end of Lake Titicaca, and about twelve miles from its present shore, are found the remains of the temple about which I have to write ;—a group of great grey blocks like another Stonehenge, but spreading over a much wider space, and interspersed with carved stones of singular design, here a doorway, there a pillar, and everywhere some mark of a great edifice long fallen into utter decay. But before going on with a description of the ruins as one finds them now, it will be as well to give some of the accounts of them. as collected by the early Spanish chroniclers.

This is what is said about them by Father Joseph de Acosta in " The Natural and Moral History of the Indies."*

This author, after describing the tradition of a great flood, says —

" The Indians say that all men were drowned in this deluge, and they " report that out of the great Lake Titicaca came one Vira Cocha, which staied " in Tiahuanaco where at this day there is to bee seene the ruines of ancient and " very strange buildings."

In another part he says :—†

" At Tiahuanaco I did measure a stone of 38 foote long, of eighteene " broad and six thicke."

Another account is by Pedro de Cieza de Leon,‡ who, after giving the

---

* Book 1, chapter xxv. Translated by Edward Grimston. Edited by Clements R. Markham, C.B., F.R.S. Hakluyt Society, 1880.

Book 6, chapter 24.   ‡ Chapter 105.

particulars of the invasion of this part of the country by Mayta Capac, in 1126, goes on thus:—

"Arrived at the Desaguadero* he ordered great canoes of rushes to be "made, in which his army passed the river, and soon subdued all the surrounding "towns. The Indians obeyed him readily, because of the wonderful reports "which they had heard of miracles performed by the Incas. Among other "towns which they reduced was one called Tiahuanaco, of whose incredibly great "edifices it will be well to say something. Among other works which are there "to cause astonishment, one of the most admirable is a hill or mound made by "the hands of man and of wonderful dimensions. Its foundations are rested on "great blocks of stone, and no one knows for what purpose the building was "put up. In another part near the mound are two figures of gigantic size, "carved in stone, and represented with long robes reaching to the ground, and "with ornamental caps upon their heads, all much injured by the effects of time "and weather, showing their great antiquity. One can also see immense walls "of stone, so large that the great wonder is how they could have been lifted by "human force and placed where they are, especially when it is known that "there are no stones of the kind in any of the hills around. One may see also "other bold edifices, and amongst them great doorways of stone, scattered "about in different parts, many of them elaborately worked and made in one "piece only in all their four dimensions, and what makes the marvel greater is "the fact that those doorways are many of them placed on stones which measure "ten yards in length, five in breadth, and two in thickness. Considering the "size of these stones, and the doorways, each made of one piece, no one can "understand how they were worked or raised, and the mind is naturally led to "think of the immense size of the stones before they were hewn into shape. "Some of the natives say about these edifices that they are works made long "before the time of the Incas; others that they were built by the same Inca "who made the Fortress of Cuzco; whilst others affirm that all these marvels "sprang from the earth in a single night."

After quoting the above account, Garcilasso de la Vega appends another on the authority of a priest named Diego de Alcobasa,† and which in Mr. Markham's translation is as follows:—

---

* The river of Lake Titicaca.

† Royal Commentaries of the Yncas, by the Ynca Garcilasso de la Vega. Translated by Clements R. Markham, Hakluyt Society, 1869.

In Tiahuanacu, in the province of Callas, amongst other things, there are some ancient ruins worthy of immortal memory. They are near the lake called by the Spaniards Chucuito, the proper name of which is Chuquivitu. Here there are some very grand edifices, and amongst them there is a square court, fifteen brazas (fathoms) each way, with walls two stories high. On one side of this court there is a hall forty-five feet long, by twenty-two broad, apparently once covered in the same way as those buildings you have seen in the house of the Sun at Cuzco, with a roof of straw. The walls, roofs, floor, and doorways are all of one single piece, carved out of a rock, and the walls of the court and of the hall are three-quarters of a yard in breadth.

The roof of the hall, though it appears to be thatch, is really of stone. For, as the Indians cover their houses with thatch, in order that this might appear like the rest, they have combed and carved the stone, so that it resembles a roof of thatch. The waters of the lake wash the walls of the court. The natives say that this and the other buildings were dedicated to the Creator of the Universe. There are also many other stones carved into the shape of men and women, so naturally that they appear to be alive, some drinking with cups in their hands, others sitting, others standing, and others walking in the stream which flows by the walls.

There are also statues of women with their infants in their laps, others with them on their backs, and in a thousand other postures. The Indians say that for the great sins of the people of those times, and because they stoned a man who was passing through the province, they were all converted into these statues.

Thus far are the words of Diego de Alcobasa, who has been a vicar and preacher to the Indians in many provinces of this kingdom.

I have put this account of Alcobasa's in smaller type to indicate that it is not to be compared in importance and accuracy with that of Cieza de Leon, who is mentioned by Humboldt with approbation.

The accounts of the solid stone chambers and the life-like statues are not found in the descriptions of other writers, nor are any traces of them visible at the present day. Alcobasa has clearly put all this down from a hearsay account, without verification by himself.

I should have been glad to refer to this writer for a confirmation of the opinion that the waters of the lake washed the walls of the temple, but this again must be the confusion of an old tradition with a contemporary account, for the battle of Huarina was fought in 1547, at a place nearer the lake and at a much lower level than Tiahuanaco, so that it would have been quite impossible for the waters to have reached the walls of the latter place, though there is reason to believe that in still more ancient times the temple could have been approached by water, and it is not improbable that the enormous stones were floated to the spot by means of barges made of reeds, after the manner of the Indians to this day.

There is one thing to be said in favour of Alcobasa's account of the great monolithic chamber, and that is that the early invaders are known to have destroyed the works of the Incas, especially such as were connected with their religion, whenever they had a good opportunity, and it was possible that by the aid of gunpowder the whole edifice was blown to pieces, perhaps, too, in the hope of finding treasure concealed beneath it.

The name of Tiahuanaco is pronounced in Tee-ah-wan-áh-co, and is said to have been given it by Mayta Ccapac, who here received a fleet Indian messenger, and commanded him to be seated, styling him huanaco, or fleet-deer—the name having that signification in the Quichua language.

But it is clear that the place must have had a name long before this, and " Chuqui a vitu " has been mentioned by one author as the old name.

It has also been called Chua-chua, and I am inclined to think either of these names more likely to be authentic than the one now borne by the place. The present name suggests the Spanish Tia (aunt) and Juana (Jane or Joan). But the matter is of little moment.

The ruins are situate in latitude 16° 22′ S., and longitude 69° 24 W.,* and are about 12,930 feet above the level of the sea, and 130 above that of Lake Titicaca, which is about twelve miles off, and is about the size of the county of Yorkshire, having no outlet except to another and smaller lake. The waters of both are brackish, but abounding with fish and wild fowl.

It now remains to describe the ruins as depicted on the various plans and sketches which are before the reader.

In Plate II. will be found a plan showing the general structural lines of the building.

Approaching from the village of Tiahuanaco, one arrives at the north-west corner of the edifice, and entering by the great monolithic doorway (marked on the plan), one finds oneself in a quadrangular space, surrounded with large stones standing on end, and arranged accurately in line. To the right is a smaller kind of court, with a sort of pavement in places, and seeming to have formed an entrance or vestibule to the greater enclosure. Beyond these walls is a hill or mound, surrounded with what remains of a wall, consisting of enormous blocks of stone. There is a pool of water, as shown near the centre of this mound, and which probably marks the spot where some treasure-seekers have ventured to open the ground, in search of the gold which the ancients generally buried in the most sacred spots.

The whole of the ruins shown on this plan occupy about the space taken

* On the authority of the Bolivian Government map, 1859.

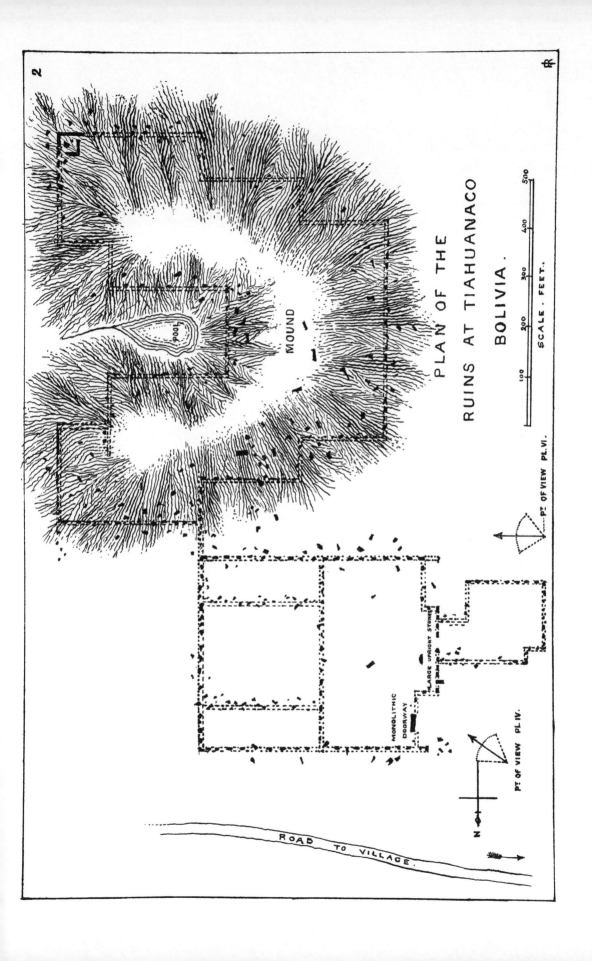

PLAN OF THE
RUINS AT TIAHUANACO
BOLIVIA.

SCALE. FEET.

100   200   300   400   500

MOUND

POOL

MONOLITHIC DOORWAY

LARGE UPRIGHT STONES

PT OF VIEW PL. VI.

PT OF VIEW PL. IV.

N

ROAD TO VILLAGE.

GROUND-PLAN OF SMALLER TEMPLE . TIAHUANACO.

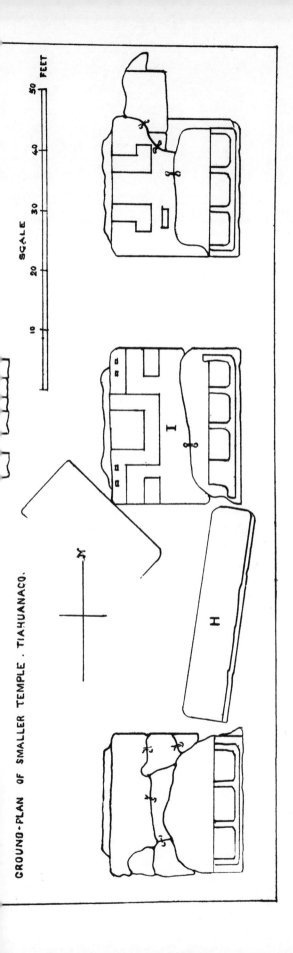

SCALE

10   20   30   40   50 FEET

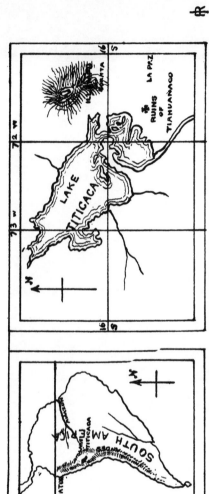

SITUATION OF RUINS WITH RESPECT TO LAKE AND CONTINENT.

up by our Houses of Parliament and Westminster Abbey put together, but there are detached smaller temples, scattered stones, and other remains spread about for nearly a square mile. The scale will give the various dimensions of the enclosures. That on the mound has been called the fortress. It contains the greatest number of displaced stones, seeming as if never finished, or if so of having served as a quarry for modern depredators, who have not always been able to carry off the stones on account of their size and weight.

PLATE III.

The smaller maps show the position of the temple with respect to Lake Titicaca and the continent of South America. The plan above them is of the foundation of a lesser temple, about a quarter of a mile from the larger one. It contains some enormous stones, which were apparently joined together with clamps of a dumb-bell shape, and the spaces for which remain, though the bronze has been removed long ago. Here is an outline of a pair of these stones, copied from a photograph by Mr. Helsby of Liverpool. The stones marked H and I (in Plate III.) are the largest in the ruins, and are shown again set on end in Plate XIX.

I made H—36 feet by 7 feet; I—26 feet by 16 feet by 6 feet, according generally with the dimensions given by Cieza de Leon, who seems to have measured these same stones. Mr. E. G. Squier gives $25\frac{1}{2}$ feet by 14 feet by $6\frac{1}{2}$ feet,[*] as the measurement, but owing to the form of the stone and the way it is half buried among others, it is difficult to get the exact dimensions.

The recesses in these stones have been compared to the seats of judges, and the whole edifice has obtained the name of the Hall of Justice.

The weight of the larger stones has been variously estimated at from 140 to 200 tons each, and the distance of the quarries from which they could have been brought at from fifteen to forty miles.

---

[*] Incidents of Travel and Exploration in the Land of the Incas, 1877.

PLATE IV.

This gives the general aspect of the ruins as approached from the north-west corner. The doorway seems as if it had been moved out of its proper place. The large upright stones are doubtless those which the early travellers thought to have formed the foundation of the ancient edifice. A notion of the size of the stones can be gained by comparing them with the figure of the man who is supposed to be six feet in height. The upright stones are of a softer kind than that forming the doorway, and they show curious remains of mortises on their upper surface, and of a kind of projecting ledge at the corners, to which Mr. Squier* has called attention, and which he conjectures to have formed a means of retaining in place the horizontal stones which formerly occupied the space between the large uprights. This arrangement is shown in the right-hand lower corner of Plate VI. The mound showing large loose stones scattered about is seen behind the row of upright stones.

PLATE V.

This represents the outside of the monolithic doorway facing the west. It is of hard trachyte, and has not suffered from the weathering of centuries so much as one might expect. Indeed the wearing away of the sharp edges does not seem so much the result of the weather as of the sand, which, in high winds, has blown about it. The niches or windows are merely deeply cut recesses in the stone, and the two lower ones doubtless had doors, with hinges of the Egyptian pattern. These have probably been of metal and have been taken away. The stone doorway has been broken into two pieces, and its present aspect gives one the idea that it has fallen or slipped some distance from its original position.

The niches may have contained images or figures, a supposition rendered likely by a passage in Salcamayhua's old account of the Antiquities of Peru,† where he mentions that one of the Incas (Apu Manco Ccapac) caused a wall to be made with three windows, which were emblems of the house of his fathers whence he descended. So that the idea of memorial windows in sacred places may be ascribed to the ancient Peruvians. But this was not the only invention of the Inca, for the same old author describes him as ordering the heads of the

---

* Incidents of Travel and Exploration in the Land of the Incas. By E. George Squier, M.A., F.S.A., 1877.
† Contained in Rites and Laws of the Yncas. Translated by C. R. Markham, C.B., F.R.S. Hakluyt Society, 1873. p. 77.

infants to be " pressed,"* that they might grow up foolish and without energy, for he thought that Indians with large round heads, being audacious in any enterprise, might also be disobedient. Whatever the reason, it is certain that the skulls, in many of the South American graves, are elongated to a great degree of deformity.

PLATE VI.

Before describing the ornaments on the inside of the great doorway, it will be well to take a glance at the possible ancient aspect of the whole exterior of the temple. The sketch in Plate VI. must be taken as an ideal representation, intended to give a general notion of the size and importance of the building as it may have formerly stood, and to show the style of architecture, as far as can be made out from the fragments which are scattered about. The vast number of imperforate windows and of niches will at once strike the observer. These seem to have been common features of the Peruvian architecture in large buildings, and may have been designed to give places for effigies, relics, and statues. As to the roof there are no means of knowing how it was constructed. I am inclined to think that the greater part of the temple was open to the sky. It is tolerably certain that the edifice was never finished, so that this ideal restoration must, in a great measure, be regarded as an indication of what may have been intended, and of the impression formed in the traveller's mind after a careful study of the remaining fragments.

FRONTISPIECE.

Returning to the monolithic doorway, the frontispiece shows its aspect from the interior of the edifice, and exhibits its eastern side, which is well covered in the upper part with sculptures, and it will be interesting to see how far their design corresponds with any of the old legends which have been handed down by the early Spanish chroniclers.†

Cristoval de Molina was a priest in the hospital of Cuzco about the middle of the sixteenth century, and had, perhaps, a better opportunity than any other writer for acquainting himself with the native legends and traditions. He thus describes the delegation of the Divine authority to the first of the Incas, and I cannot but regard the sculptures on this doorway as an attempt to perpetuate the same tradition, to which it corresponds in so many material points.

* Rites and Laws. p. 78.
† The Fables and Rites of the Incas. Translated by Clements R. Markham, C B., F.R.S., Hakluyt Society, 1873.

This is what Molina has to say :—" But in a house of the Sun, called " Poquen Cancha, which is near Cuzco, they had the life of each one of the " Yncas, with the lands they conquered, painted with figures on certain boards, " and also their origin. Among these paintings the following fable was repre-" sented—

" In the life of Manco Ccapac, who was the first Inca, and from whom " they began to be called the Children of the Sun, they had a full account of the " deluge. They say that all people and all created things perished in it, inso-" much that the water rose above all the highest mountains in the world. No " living things survived except a man and a woman, who remained in a box, and " when the waters subsided the wind carried them to Huanaco,* which will be " over seventy leagues from Cuzco, a little more or less. The Creator of all " things commanded them to remain there as *mitimas*;† and there, in Tiahuanaco, " the Creator began to raise up the people and nations that are in that region, " making one of each nation of clay, and painting the dresses that each one was " to wear. Those that wear their hair, with hair; and those that were to be " shorn, with hair cut; and to each nation was given the language that was to " be spoken, and the songs to be sung, and the seeds and food that they were " to sow. When the Creator had finished painting and making the said nations " and figures of clay, he gave life and soul to each one, as well men as women, " and ordered that they should pass under the earth. Thence each nation came " up in the places to which he ordered them to go. Thus they say that some " came out of caves, others issued from hills, others from fountains, others from " the trunks of trees. From this cause, and owing to having come forth and " commenced to multiply from those places, and to having had the beginning of " their lineage in them, they made *huacas* ‡ and places of worship of them in " memory of the origin of their lineage, which proceeded from them. Thus " each nation uses the dress with which they invest their *huaca*, and they say " that the first that was born from that place was there turned into stones, others " say the first of their lineages were turned into falcons, condors, and other " animals and birds. Hence the *huacas* they use and worship are in different " shapes.

" There are other nations which say that when the deluge came all people " were destroyed except a few who escaped on hills, in caves, or trees, and that

---

* Tiahuanaco.   † Colonists or settlers.   ‡ Sacred thing or place ; idol.

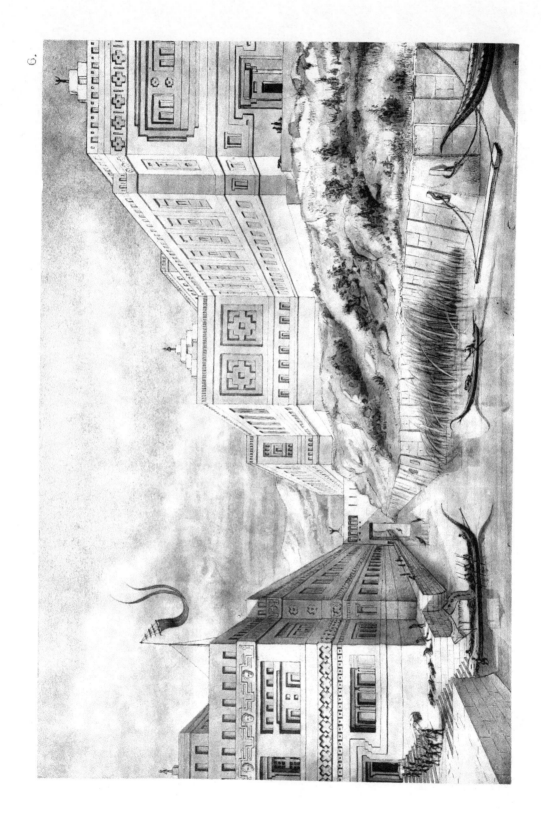

" these were very few, but that they began to multiply, and that, in memory of
" the first of their race who escaped in such places, they made idols of stone,
" giving the name of him who had thus escaped to each *huaca*. Thus each
" nation worshipped and offered sacrifices of such things as they used. There
" were, however, some nations who had a tradition of a Creator of all things.
" They made some sacrifices to him, but not in such quantity or with so much
" veneration as to their idols or *huacas*. But to return to the fable. They say
" that the Creator was in Tiahuanaco, and that there was his chief abode, hence
" the superb edifices worthy of admiration in that place. On these edifices were
" painted many dresses of Indians, and there were many stones in the shape of
" men and women who had been changed into stone for not obeying the com-
" mands of the Creator."

It seems clear to me that the sculptures on the gateway were intended to
represent the Creator delivering His mandates to the different heads of tribes as
described in the legend handed down by Molina. We see a crowned, sceptred,
and enthroned figure of large size extending his sceptres towards a number of
other crowned and kneeling figures on each side of him. Some of the latter have
the heads of condors, all have sceptres or emblems of authority, and the whole
design corresponds with what might have been expected from a primitive artist
if ordered to depict the scene just quoted from Molina's narrative.

In describing the figures more in detail, I shall show other points which
make it almost certain that this was the object intended to be represented.

It will be seen that there are rectangular mortise holes in the doorway,
and which seem to have been designed to take the ends of beams.

The masonry is excellent throughout, and all the lines are as straight, the
angles as square, and the surfaces as level as would be produced by any good
workman of the present day.

The art is rather devoted to indicate than to imitate, and corresponds in
style with other monuments which were designed to perpetuate the memory of
some legend of faith or mode of worship.

The size of the monolith, according to Mr. Squier's* measurements, is as
follows :—

(The measures which agree substantially with those made by me, refer
only to the part above ground). The outside dimensions are—

* Peru. Incidents of Travel and Exploration in the Land of the Incas. By E. G. Squier 1877.

13 feet 5 inches by 7 feet 2 inches by 1 foot 6 inches (thickness).

The opening of the doorway is 4 feet 6, by 2 feet 9.

It is much to be regretted that the whole stone has not been examined, as it could then be seen if it consisted of a perforated block (which I believe) or of the uprights and top portion only.

The good curate of Tiahuanaco (I thank him now for his kindness and hospitality) told me that it was commonly supposed that the blocks were not stone at all, but of a kind of cement. Without believing this, I must admit having seen artificial stones so closely resembling natural ones that it would be difficult to distinguish the difference. With an unknown number of centuries in which to harden, it is possible to conceive some of these fragments as having been moulded rather than carved. I saw no mark of chisel in any of the stones.

PLATE VII.

This is a larger representation of the central figure over the doorway, somewhat restored as regards definition, the original being much weather-worn but showing more or less distinctly all the features given in the drawing. (The drawing is to a scale of one-fourth the lineal dimensions of the original)

At first sight the figure appears of the very rudest, but on looking at it more attentively one can find many symbols and accessories introduced which correspond with the primitive ideas of majesty and of deity. That this was intended for a figure of the Creator I have (after perusing Molina's account) no manner of doubt. The sceptre and the throne express the idea of dominion and authority, the six heads round the waist imply the power of taking vengeance, the two heads hung from the arms convey perhaps the notion of Divine skill or craft-mastery. On the crown are puma's heads, showing the idol as lord over the strongest and fiercest animals. The rays round the face perhaps allude to the Sun, the second object of the people's worship, and the source of their life and prosperity. The marks on the cheeks may be meant for tears, rudely indicating the compassion which, as a god-like attribute, they might have intended to represent. The heads of the birds on the sceptre in his left hand are those of parrots, and it is most likely that this was the artist's way of showing that the *Vira Cocha*, the " soul of the universe," was giving speech and language to the different tribes—just as described in Molina's document, already given at length. The bird's head upon the sceptre in the right hand of the figure is that of a condor, the type of swiftness and power.

The marks on the dress seem rudely to indicate plants and seeds, leading one to the ideas of fertility and increase for which in their prayers the Incas did not omit to ask. Altogether the figure is such as a highly-skilled mason (but who had never seen a work of sculpture) might be expected to produce if ordered to make an image of an ideal character, who was to be conceived as lord over men and nature, distributing sceptres, and dominating kings, and endowed with all the attributes of power and majesty suitable to impress the minds of primitive worshippers.

Whether the figure was ever covered with thin plates of gold, after the manner of the other sacred effigies, must remain in doubt. The high relief of the sculpture would have allowed of its being so adorned by hammering the plates round its edges. But there is no definite evidence of its having been so treated.

The throne is ornamented with a curious design of some merit, and contains representations of the heads of parrots and monkeys, two creatures having man-like powers of mimicry, and so, perhaps, distinguished with the honour of acting as " supporters " to the throne.

The design on the central part of the throne is very like Japanese art.

It is only fair to observe that in Mr. Squier's* drawing of this figure there is no representation of the six heads round the waist. I certainly drew them on the spot as heads, and I am confirmed by referring to D'Orbigny's great work,† and finding that in 1837 he distinctly depicted them in the same way that I have done. I had not seen D'Orbigny's work when I made the sketch.

In this monument one seems to see the first merging of pure nature-worship into the adoration of a more personal object of devotion, and this corresponds with what might be expected in the pictured decorations of perhaps one of the earliest temples ever raised in honour of a personal Deity. To those who have found a difficulty in believing that ideas of primitive religion were exclusively communicated to any one country, or even hemisphere, this stone with its traditions will be a testimony that such ideas, like the sunlight itself, have compassed the whole curcuit of the earth.

---

* Peru, &c. E. G. Squier, 1877. † D'Orbigny. Voyage dans l'Amerique Meridionale.

PLATE VIII.

These are larger drawings of the figures on each side of the central one. They are somewhat restored, as on account of there being a great many alike it was easy to find in one what the effects of time and weather had obliterated in another. (The drawings are to a scale of one-half the lineal dimensions of the original.)

The first figure represents a winged human figure with the head of a condor. It is crowned and holds a divided sceptre in its hand. It kneels in apparent adoration of the central figure. Its ornaments consist for the most part of the heads of fishes. It is probable that these figures represent the chiefs of some nation bordering the lake. The head is marked as that of the condor by the sort of warty appendage under the eye which may be seen in any living specimen of the bird. Note also the wavy line dividing the beak.

Garcilasso de la Vega* says that: "An Indian is not looked upon as " honourable unless he is descended from a fountain, river, or lake (or even the " sea), or from a wild animal, such as a bear, lion, tiger, eagle, or the bird they " call a cuntur (condor), or some other bird of prey; or from a mountain, cave, " or forest, each one as he fancies, for the better praise and glory of his name "

In a narrative by Francisco de Avila,† a condor is mentioned as speaking and being made sacred.

Birds with women's heads are also spoken of by Molina.‡

The other figure in the plate represents a winged and crowned human figure of much the same character. He also holds a sceptre. This staff had a name (Tupac Yavri), and was supposed to have been miraculously turned into fine gold in the hands of the first Inca.§

PLATE IX.

This is a portion of the ornament which runs along the base of the other figures. Like the last drawings, it is restored by collating the more perfect parts, as it is even more damaged by time and weather than they are. (The scale is one-third lineal.)

It suggests the Greek form of ornament, and it is profusely adorned with

---

* Royal Commentaries, Book I. Translated by C. R. Markham for the Hakluyt Society, 1867.

† Translated by C. R. Markham, C.B., F.R.S., for the Hakluyt Society, in Rites and Laws of the Yncas, 1873.

‡ Account of the Fables and Rites of the Incas, by Cristoval de Molina. Translated by C. R. Markham for the Hakluyt Society, 1873.

§ Salcamayhua. Antiquities of Peru, in "Rites and Laws of the Yncas." Translated by C. R. Markham. Hakluyt Society, 1873.

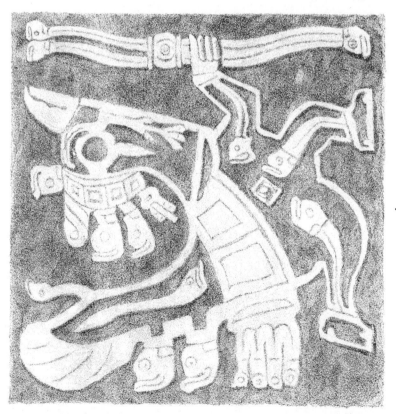

A

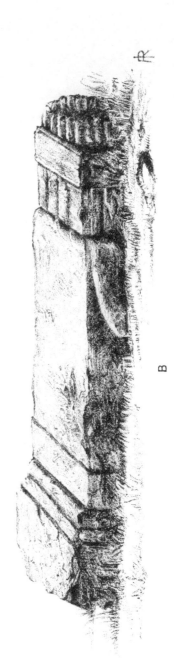

B

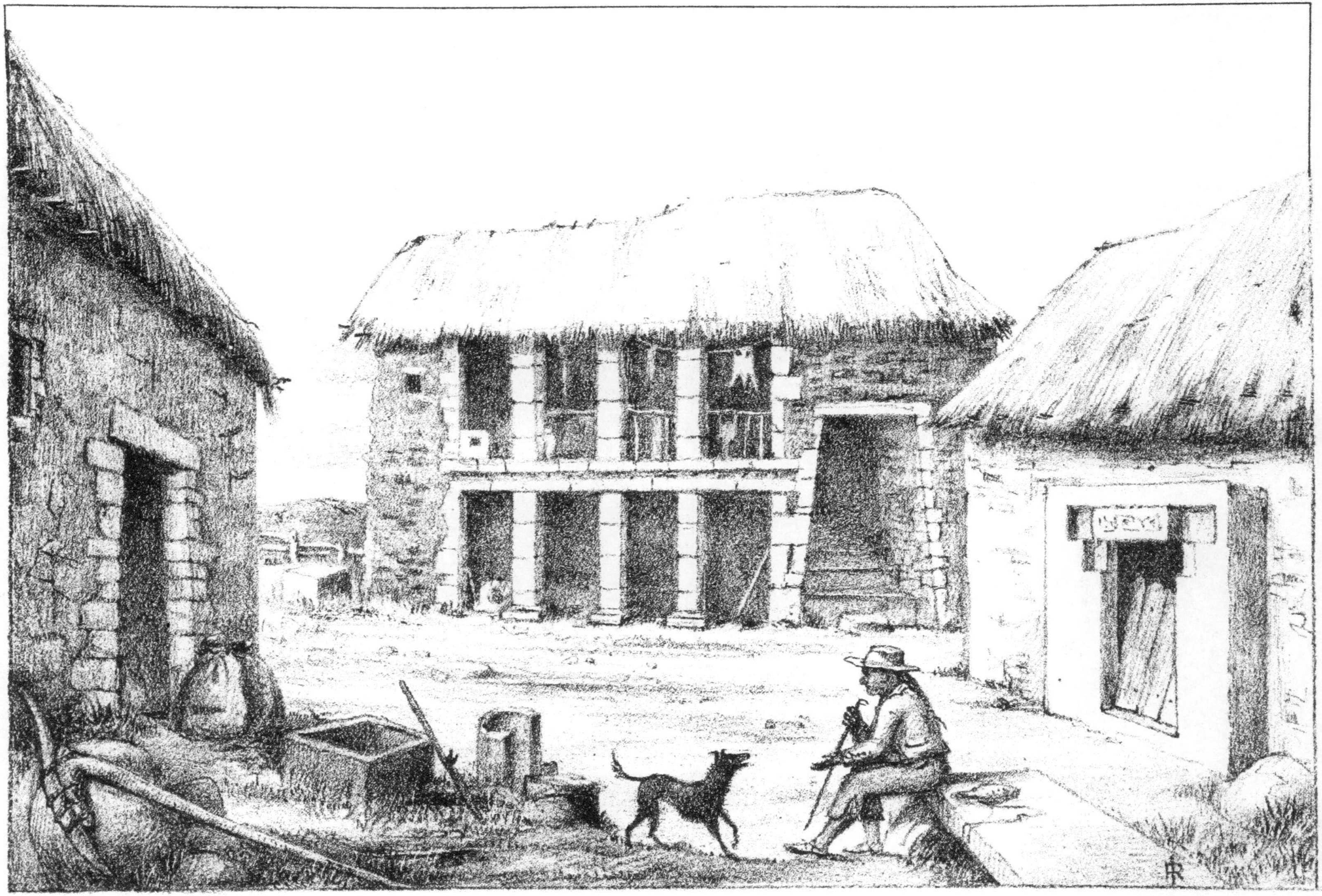

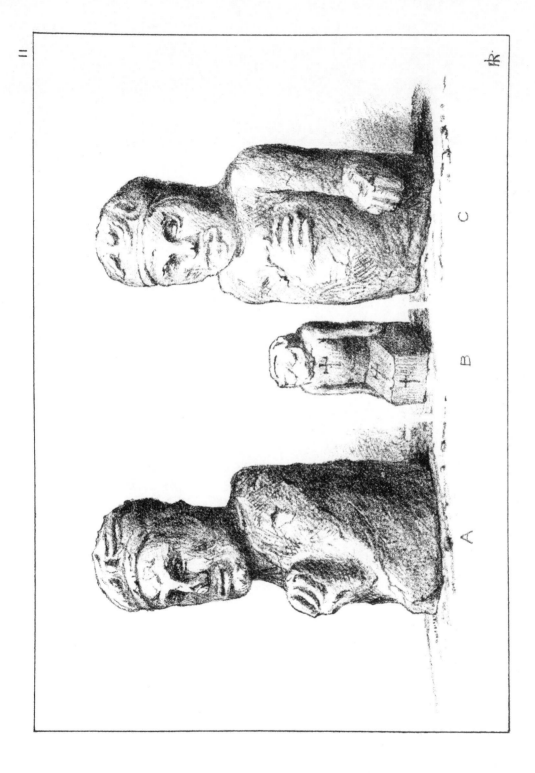

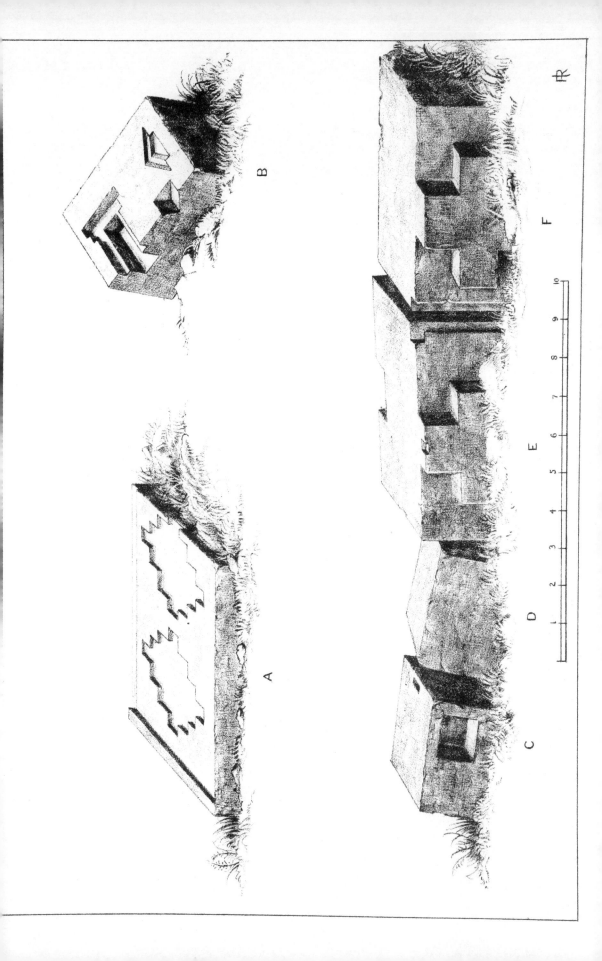

A B C D E F G H I K

1 2 3 4 5 6 7 8 9 10 FEET

representations of the heads of birds and fishes, with human faces like suns at intervals. Some of the faces have marks on the cheeks like the tears on the central figure. The design is not without ingenuity and merit. It may have been intended for a rude representation of a serpent with many heads, and if so, this quaint stone furnishes us with an illustration of the rude form of serpent-worship, which had at an early period found a footing among the ancient Peruvians. Mr. James Ferguson has indicated the probability of such being the case.[*]

It is recorded by Garcilasso de la Vega[†] that before the time of the Incas " they venerated the great serpents that are met with in the Antis[‡]—twenty-five " to thirty feet in length, more or less, and thicker than a man's thigh—for their " monstrous size and fierceness."

B. is a prostrate idol lying on its face near the ruins.

It is about 9 feet in length, and of a style of art apparently but little later than that of the monolithic doorway.

Here is a rough sketch of a head[§] depicted in Rivero and Tschndi's work and which, although I have not seen the stone, it will be well to describe it here as it seems to belong to this period and style of art.

The stone is situated on the road to La Paz, and about four leagues from the rest of the ruins.

" The head of one of these statues is 3 feet 6 inches long, from the point of " the beard to the upper part of the ornamental head dress ; and from the nose to the back " of the head it measures 2 feet 7 inches. It is adorned with a species of round cap, 1 foot " 7 inches high and 2 feet 5 inches in width. In the upper part are certain wide vertical bands, and in the " lower are symbolical figures with human faces. From the eyes, which are large and round, two wide bands, " each with three double circles, project to the chin. From the outer part of each eye a band descends, " adorned with two squares, terminating in a serpent. The nose is slightly prominent, surrounded on the " lower side by a wide semi-circular band, and terminating towards the inner side of the eyes in two corners. " The mouth forms a transverse oval, garnished with sixteen teeth. From the under lip project, in the form " of a beard, six bands, towards the edge of the chin. The ear is represented by a semi-lunar figure in a " square, and in the fore part of it is a vertical band with three squares terminating in the head of a wild " beast. On the neck there are many human figures. The sculpture of this head is very remarkable."

PLATE X.

This represents the hut of what would be considered a wealthy Indian farmer of the vicinity.

It is given to show how the ancient stones have been used in building it.

---

[*] Tree and Serpent-Worship, 1873.　　　　　　[†] Royal Commentaries, 1-9.
[‡] Eastward tropical forests.　　　　　　[§] Antiguedades Peruanas, p. 295.

All the well squared stones of the pillars and stairway as well as the fine doorway on the spectator's right, have been taken from the ruins. The latter doorway, I think, must have belonged to the "hall of justice," described in Plate III. It consists of one stone accurately perforated through its centre.

To what extent this spoliation of the ruins has been carried on for centuries it is difficult now to tell, but it is certain that for many miles round, the temple has supplied dressed stones to be used wherever the form of masonry required a better class of work than the natives are now able or willing to produce. It is very certain that since the time of the early Spanish chroniclers much havoc has been made among the more accurately cut stones which have been found so suitable for building purposes that some of them have been carried even as far as La Paz, where they form part of the Cathedral. The difficulty of again finding stones which have been so used is instanced by the state of the Great Pyramid, where it is known that whole acres of the hard and polished casing-stones have disappeared, yet it would be difficult in Cairo to find a score of them built into the modern city.

PLATE XI.

These are stone idols or images, and the two larger ones are placed one on each side of the modern church door. They are about five feet in height, and of a totally different style of art to that of the other figures. I think they must belong to a much later period when art had become more imitative and less symbolic than at the time when the great doorway was carved. The smaller figure is of a more severe type, and may belong to the older period. It is ornamented with crosses, but it is presumed they have been the work of the moderns. In place of a hand the figure has a rude face carved on the lower part of the arm, probably a rude symbol of artistic or mechanical skill. The legend about these stones is given in Salcamayhua's* narrative.

In describing the journeys of Tonapa, a bearded man, who went about preaching virtue and morality, when he came to Tiahuanaco. "They say that " the people of that town were engaged in drinking and dancing when Tonapa " came to them, and they did not listen to him. Then out of pure anger he " denounced them in the language of the land, and when he departed from the " place all the people who were dancing were turned into stones, and they may " be seen to this day."

* Rites and Laws of the Incas, p. 73.

This reminds one of Smith, the weaver's,* expression in Shakespeare:—
" And the bricks are alive at this day to testify it, therefore deny it not "

Molina (who is generally to be preferred) gives a legend on the same subject.

PLATE XII.

These are various curiously carved stones found scattered about the ruins. The workmanship is so good and the stones are so well preserved that one cannot avoid the impression of being in the mason's yard where a great modern building is in course of erection. The squareness and correctness of the work is quite wonderful, and when one considers that the tools used were probably only harder stones set in handles, or bronze bars, which would not take a strong, fine edge, the wonder is increased.

Some of the larger stones, having a projecting cross on the face, might have served for season-dials to mark the time of the solstices or to indicate festivals, ploughing time or other periods. I am sorry I did not make more accurate measures so as to throw more light on this point, which did not occur to me at the time. It is easy to see that the face of the cross being placed towards the east or west the length of the shadow of its upper edge at noon as projected on the horizontal arm would vary with the time of year, and perhaps on reaching some particular mark or angle give indication of the times connected with the sowing of crops, planting, shearing, breeding of sheep, and other simple agricultural work. If placed towards the north the shadow may have served to divide the day.

Some of the recesses of curious form might have had a similar object.

It is recorded that the Spanish invaders when robbing the palaces and temples, demolished the pillars for denoting the time of the solstices, believing them to be the idols of the Indians.†

PLATE XIII.

More stones of a similar nature, and of fine workmanship.

A has a circle drawn apparently with compasses.

B seems to have formed part of a doorway.

C‡ is a round stone like a grindstone. There is mention in a legend quoted by Avila of a toad with two heads found under a grindstone.

* Henry VI. Part 2, 4-2.
† Cuzco, a journey to the ancient capital of Peru, by C. R. Markham, p. 138.
‡ Rites and Laws of the Incas, p. 137.

I is an accurately finished stone which formed part of a water conduit.

K seems like part of a causeway or landing stage, and seemed to me to be water worn, although it is difficult to be certain on the point.

This is what Mr. E. G. Squier* says of the character of the masonry generally :—" I may say once for all, carefully weighing my words, that in no " part of the world have I seen stones cut with such admirable skill as in Peru, " and in no part of Peru are there any to surpass those which are scattered " over the plains at Tiahuanaco."

PLATE XIV.

Further instances of good masonry among the myriad fragments scattered about.

A seems to have been the lid or cover of some aperture. It has two handles neatly undercut.

B is a window of trachyte of careful workmanship, and made in one piece.

D and E are two views of a corner piece to some stone conduit, which is carefully ornamented with projecting lines. The aqueducts of the Incas† were described as the most important works of irrigation ever accomplished in the world. They reached in some cases to over a hundred leagues in length, and gave life to the parched lands in the western part of the country.

After the conquest they were allowed to go out of repair, and so vast tracts of pasture land became again barren.

PLATE XV.

Another series of detached fragments with various kinds of niches, mouldings and projections.

The stone E is curious as showing an accurately cut depression with miniature steps leading down to it in various places. These. steps being but two or three inches in height, preclude the notion that they were ever intended for use by human beings, and support the theory which has been suggested. of the stone being a kind of architect's model of some larger structure.

The slab may be the remains of some altar, font, or sacrificial stone, and this supposition is supported by the form of the Egyptian altars, which have been found similarly provided with steps in miniature (*see* next Plate A).

* Peru, Travel and Exploration in the Land of the Incas, p. 279.
† Royal Commentaries. G. de la Vega, bk. v.

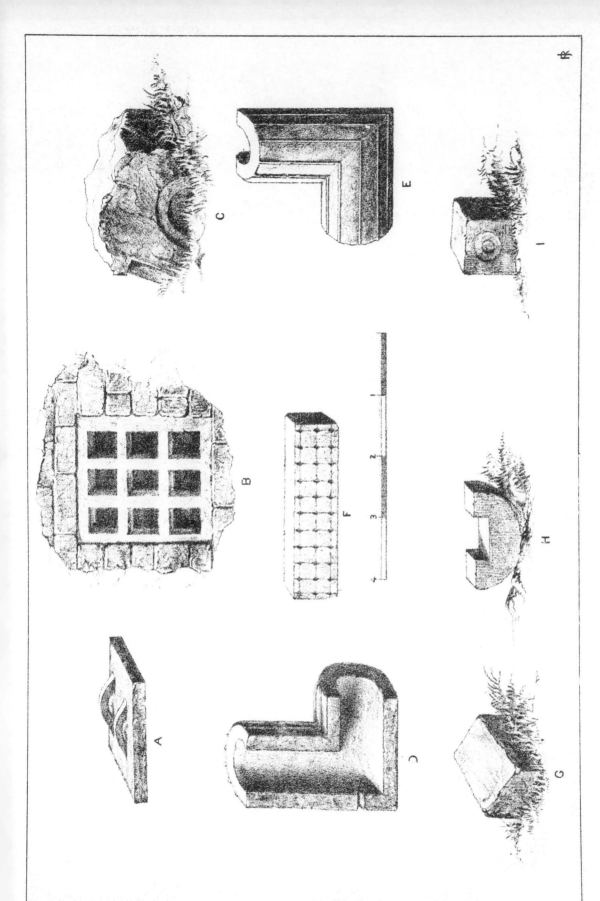

A

B

C

D

E

|' 2 3 4 5 6 7 8 9 10|
FEET

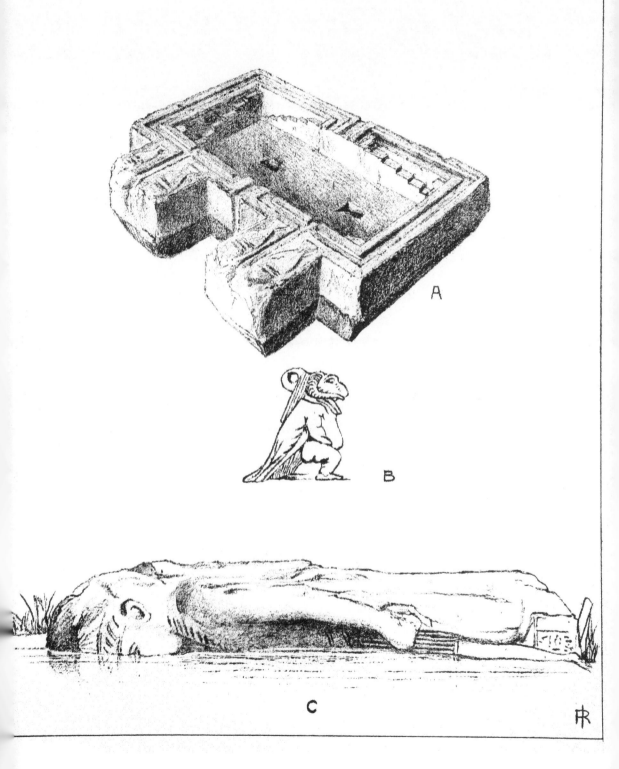

A

B

C

ᴀꞞ

A

E

B

C

D

In favour of its being a font is the following passage from Salcomayhua,* in which he even gives the name of the stone used for the purpose of a kind of baptism. " It is said that the Ynca sent men to search for the place called " Titicaca where the great Tonapa had arrived, and that they brought water " thence to pour over the infant Ynca Ruca, while they celebrated the praises " of Tonapa.†   In the spring on the top of the rocks the water was in a basin‡ " called *ccapacchama quispisutuc unu* (words signifying rich—joy—crystal drops " —water).   Future Yncas caused this water to be brought in a bowl called curi- " ccacca (Golden Rock), and placed before them in the middle of the Square of " Cuzco called Huacay Pata Cusi-pata, where they did honour to the water that " had been touched by Tonapa."

Molina also names a ceremonial in which a similar stone might find a place.

" He (the Ynca) had a great vase of gold containing Chicha.§   It was " received by the priest, who emptied it into the urn which, as has been said, " is like a stone fountain plated with gold.   This urn had a hole made in such a " way that the Chicha could enter a pipe or sewer passing under the ground to " the houses of the Sun, the thunder, and the Creator."

The stone may have been used as a sacrificial altar, as we are informed by the old chroniclers that the Peruvians sacrificed sheep to their deity, and that these sheep had to be the finest and most perfect of the flock.

That bathing had a part too in their religion, we see from the account of Molina, where he describes that on a certain feast day in August they had bathings in rivers, accompanied by prayers for health, and on this day no quarrelling or anger was permitted and all the poor were well fed.

It is curious thus to notice at how many points the religious system of the Peruvians came into contact with Egyptian, Jewish and Mohammedan, and even Christian observances.

PLATE XVI.

These are Egyptian relics which I have introduced, as showing strong points of analogy with those of Peru.   A is a stone in the British Museum, described as a sacrificial altar with vases of libation.   It has miniature steps leading down to it in the same way as the Peruvian stone depicted on Plate

---

* Rites and Laws of the Incas, p. 87.   † Molina also names a ceremonial.
‡ Rites and Laws of the Incas, p. 25.   § Maize-beer.

XV. The Egyptian stone, however, is much smaller, being only about 21 inches by 11.

B is a figure (copied from a drawing by Miss Emily Sharpe) which shows the peculiar mixture of the animal and human forms, indulged in equally by the Egyptians and the Peruvians—compare with Plate VIII.

C is a prostrate statue which I sketched at Memphis, and which forms an eastern counterpart to the idol depicted in Plate IX.

PLATE XVII.

A represents a smaller monolithic doorway, about 7 feet 6 inches in height, and having a running ornament (nearly defaced by time) across the top. It has, like the greater doorway, mortises accurately cut, as if for the insertion of timber.

B is a basalt jar brought by me from Tiahuanaco, and it is decorated with the same kind of heads and style of ornament as that of the great gateway in Plate VI. Inside it shows the fine circular marks of the tool with which it was bored out, and which probably consisted of some harder stone fixed in a rude kind of lathe.

C is a smaller stone pot, without decoration. Both the above are now in the British Museum.

D and E are modern jars, as used among the Indians, and which give evidence of a survival of the ancient type.

Immense quantities of broken earthen pottery are found about the ruins.

PLATE XVIII.

A is an image about 3 feet in height, and which is propped against a garden wall. It seems to have had a head like that of an eagle. It has also a face carved in the place of the hand.

Molina mentions an engle and a falcon carved in stone.

B is a low-relief slab in the *plaza*, or market-place. It is much weather-worn, and seems to represent the same figure as that depicted over the great doorway.

PLATE XIX.

This shows at one view the principal monoliths of the world, drawn to the same scale so as to give a good idea of their comparative sizes.

A is the monster obelisk of St. John, Lateran, in Rome. Its height is 105 feet 4 inches, and its weight about 454 tons.

B is the Luxor obelisk, in Paris, measuring 76 feet 4 inches in height, and weighing about 246 tons.

C is Cleopatra's Needle, in New York, the one which for so many centuries formed a landmark at Alexandria. It is 68 feet 11 inches high, and weighs about 186 tons.*

D is Cleopatra's other Needle, now on the Thames Embankment, London. It is 68 feet 5½ inches in height, and weighs about 186 tons.†

E. The great statue of Osymandius at Thebes, probably by far the largest stone ever moved by human agency, and which cannot have weighed much less than 2,500 tons.

F is the monster statue of Memnon, and is the one which was supposed to utter a voice at the rising of the Sun.

G. The roof of the tomb of Theoderic, at Ravenna, in Italy. It is placed edgewise in the drawing.

H and I are two stones from Tiahuanaco, the same as shewn in the plan of the smaller temple in Plate III. The stone H weighs about 170 tons. A man, 6 feet high, is shewn as standing before it.

K is the principal trilithon at Stonehenge.

L is one of the largest stones of modern London, being one of those at the base of the fine Doric columns in Hardwick's grand portico to the Euston Square Station.

These megaliths from other parts may serve to give a good notion of the comparative size of the stones in Tiahuanaco, which, though perhaps larger than any stones quarried and wrought in Europe or Asia, do not rival those of Ancient Egypt.

I have now done "that which I could attain unto," in calling attention to these fine relics of early civilization in the western world, and I am much in debt to the various authors and translators whose remarks I have found it absolutely necessary to quote. There is, however, one author yet to be cited— Alexander von Humboldt,‡ who says about these ruins—

"It were to be wished that some learned traveller could visit the banks

---

* The dimensions of the first three obelisks are from Rondelets "Art de Batir."
† As measured and calculated by Mr. Waynman Dixon.   ‡ Vues des Cordilliéres.

" of the great lake of Titicaca, the province of Collas, and more especially the
" elevated plain of Tiahuanaco, which is the centre of an ancient civilization in
" South America.   On that spot there still exist some remains of those edifices
" which Pedro de Cieza has described with great simplicity, they seem never to
" have been finished, and at the arrival of the Spaniards the natives attributed
" the construction of them to a race of white or bearded men who inhabited the
" ridge of the Cordilleras long before the foundation of the empire of the Incas."

The task suggested by the venerable traveller yet remains to be done in
the minute completeness which would have satisfied so exact a man.   It may be
broadly stated that no explorations worthy of the name have yet been made
there.   A few treasure seekers have dug pits here and there, but as gold only
was their object it is not likely that anything of antiquarian interest arrested
their attention for a moment.

It may happen that in an interval of peace some traveller will be found
with the means, time and inclination to make some definite efforts towards the
further unravelling of this ancient stone riddle.

20, Bartholomew Villas,
              London, N.W.
     January, 1884.

A

B

THE GREAT MONOLITHS OF THE WORLD.

INDEX.

		PAGE.
Acosta	9, 13
Alcobasa	15
Altars...	28, 29
Ancestor Worship	7
Anecdote of the Inca	8
Animals	24
Aqueducts	28
Avila	27
Baptism	29
Bathing	29
Cieza de Leon	13
Cleopatra's Needles	31
Coca-chewing	11
Condors	21, 24
Conduits	28
Creator	8, 29

		PAGE.
Deluge	20
Dials	27
Dixon, W.	31
Doorway, Monolithic	18
Doorway, Smaller Monolithic	30
Doorway, Size of	22
D'Orbigny	18, 23
Egyptian Relics	29
Embalming the Dead	9
Emblems	22
Evans and Askin	11
Fergusson, Jas.	25
Fishes	24
Font	29
Frontispiece, Description of	19

INDEX—*continued.*

	PAGE.
Garcilasso de la Vega	8, 25
Gold, Fondness for	6
Gold-plates	23, 29
Greek Style of Ornament	24
Grindstone	27
Hall of Justice	17
Heads Deformed	18, 19
Humboldt	15, 31
Idols	25, 26, 30
Incas	6, 29
Indian Characteristics	11
Jars	30
La Paz, Cathedral of	26
Large Stones	31
Lateran Obelisk, Rome	31
Latitude of Tiahuanaco	16
London Obelisk	31
Longitude of Tiahuanaco	16
Maize-beer	29
Manco Ccapac, the Good Inca	9
Markham, C. R.	8
Masonry	21, 28
Memnon, Statue of	31

	PAGE.
Memorial Windows	18
Memphis, Statue at	30
Modern Depredations	26
Molina	19, 29, 30
Monoliths of the World	30
New York Obelisk	31
Niches	18
Obelisks	31
Ornamental Frieze	24
Pacha Camac	8
Paris Obelisk	31
Peruvian Race, Decay of	7
Peruvian Religion	7
Pizarro	6
Portico at Euston Square	31
Pottery	30
Prayers	8, 9
Prescott, W. H.	5
Primitive Religion	23
Pronunciation of Tiahuanaco	16
Protesters against Pizarro's Conduct	6
Pyramid	26
Restoration, Ideal	19
Rites	29

INDEX—*continued.*

	PAGE.
Rivero and Tschudi	25
Roof	19
Royal Commentaries of the Incas...	9, 10, 14, 24
Ruins, Position of	13
Sacrifices	8
Salcamayhua	18, 24, 26
Season-Dials	27
Serpent-Worship	25
Size of Buildings	16
Size of Stones	17, 31
Slab, Carved	30
Squier, E. G.	18
Smaller Temple	17
Statues	15
Stonehenge	31
Sun-Gods Charge to the First Inca ...	10
Sun-Worship	7
Symbols	22

	PAGE.
Temple, Smaller	17
Thebes, Statue at	31
Theoderic, Tomb of	31
Throne	23
Tiahuanaco, Elevation of	16
Tiahuanaco, Origin of Name	16
Tiahuanaco, Pronunciation of Name ...	16
Time-Pillars	27
Titicaca Lake	12, 13, 15
Titicaca, Size of	16
Tonapa	26
Tradition ... ·	20
Treasure-Seekers	16, 32
Water, Reaching Ruins...	15
Weight of Stones	17, 31
Workmanship	26
Venus...	9

For EU product safety concerns, contact us at Calle de José Abascal, 56–1°, 28003 Madrid, Spain or eugpsr@cambridge.org.

www.ingramcontent.com/pod-product-compliance
Ingram Content Group UK Ltd.
Pitfield, Milton Keynes, MK11 3LW, UK
UKHW030856150625
459647UK00021B/2788